YOUR KNOWLEDGE HAS VALUE

- We will publish your bachelor's and master's thesis, essays and papers

- Your own eBook and book - sold worldwide in all relevant shops

- Earn money with each sale

Upload your text at www.GRIN.com
and publish for free

Bibliographic information published by the German National Library:

The German National Library lists this publication in the National Bibliography; detailed bibliographic data are available on the Internet at http://dnb.dnb.de .

This book is copyright material and must not be copied, reproduced, transferred, distributed, leased, licensed or publicly performed or used in any way except as specifically permitted in writing by the publishers, as allowed under the terms and conditions under which it was purchased or as strictly permitted by applicable copyright law. Any unauthorized distribution or use of this text may be a direct infringement of the author s and publisher s rights and those responsible may be liable in law accordingly.

Imprint:

Copyright © 2017 GRIN Verlag
Print and binding: Books on Demand GmbH, Norderstedt Germany
ISBN: 9783668704015

This book at GRIN:

https://www.grin.com/document/417398

Daniel Tonga

Xenophobia and its impact on culture integration. A critical analysis of Zambia's case

GRIN Verlag

GRIN - Your knowledge has value

Since its foundation in 1998, GRIN has specialized in publishing academic texts by students, college teachers and other academics as e-book and printed book. The website www.grin.com is an ideal platform for presenting term papers, final papers, scientific essays, dissertations and specialist books.

Visit us on the internet:

http://www.grin.com/

http://www.facebook.com/grincom

http://www.twitter.com/grin_com

Xenophobia and its impact on culture integration: a critical analysis of Zambia's case

Daniel Tonga
Journalist, Media Consultant and Economist 274/4 Chawama, Lusaka, Zambia

Abstract

Over the last 50 years, Zambia has never experienced xenophobia or any form of social instability, a record of which made the country become known as a beacon of peace worldwide. However, one of the most horrific incidents took place in 2016, when two foreigners were burnt alive in the capital, Lusaka by a mob of local residents angered by a presence of foreigners. This hostility towards foreigners spread across some parts of the country and resulted in a destruction of shops and businesses owned by foreigners. A series of these events came to be known as xenophobia. The incidences of xenophobia were widely covered by the media and had a huge impact on culture integration and the country's image. Zambia's experience of xenophobia affected peace and remains a threat to cultural integration despite the country remaining home to refugees, asylum seekers and immigrants coming from Rwanda, Zimbabwe, Somalia and the Democratic Republic of Congo. This study aims at assessing xenophobia, its predicates, causes and effects. Thus, the paper examines and critically analyses xenophobia and its impact on cultural integration in Zambia's case.

Keywords: *Culture; Integration; Xenophobia; Ritual Killings; Media; Communications, Foreigners; Host Country and Image*

1.0 Introduction

Zambia has been known as a beacon of peace around the world because of the social and cultural stability it has enjoyed since gaining independence from Britain in 1964.Since then, the country has gone through political, economic, social and cultural changes. Despite these changes, the country has remained an amalgamation of 70 endogenous diverse tribal groups with a growing number of foreign cultural groups. Even with growing number of foreigners, the country has been able to transition for years without any social or cultural problems.

Over the years, the number of foreigners getting into the country has increased tremendously leading to cultural diversity. Among the leading causes of foreigners getting into Zambia has been growing political instability and wars in countries within Southern Africa. These experiences have led people to flee their home countries for peace and have settled in Zambia. This has created a blend of cultures which is a hallmark feature of contemporary Zambia.

According to United Nations High Commissioner for Refugees UNHCR Report(2015)indicates that 42,500 people were forced to flee their home countries per day due to conflict and persecution. As a result, Zambia has been home to foreigners and now hosting refugees from Zimbabwe, Angola, Mozambique, the Democratic Republic of Congo, Burundi and Rwanda.

This situation has led to a composition of different cultures in Zambia. Apart from foreigners crossing over to Zambia as a result of conflicts, instability and war from their home countries, some have migrated for economic reasons and opportunities with hopes of integrating into the Zambian society permanently. Yakushko (2009) observed that economic imbalance pulls individuals toward countries with prospects of higher earnings or sheer survival. However, in early 2016 the influx of foreigners became a daunting challenge for most indigenous people.

The problem of foreigners was compounded by increasing economic challenges the country faced such as high unemployment, lack of economic opportunities and extreme poverty. During this period, a belief emerged that prevailing economic challenges and pressure were caused by an influx of foreigners taking up employment, business opportunities and economic advantage over local residents.

This prejudice was not different from Fritzsche (1994) who observed that prejudice against immigrants can offer an emotional outlet for fear when both the internal and external affairs of a country are unstable. Furthermore, during the period of economic downturn, the country experienced a series of ritual killings and these killings were believed to have been carried out by foreigners. This heightened hatred towards foreigners which caused local residents to attack foreigners leading to a wave of xenophobia. Foreigners targeted in the attack included Rwandans, Zimbabweans and Somalians. Shops and businesses belonging to foreigners were looted by local residents, an indication that these acts were purely for economic reasons.

According to scape-goating hypothesis of xenophobia Allport (1954), foreigner is used as a scapegoat, someone to blame for social ills and personal frustrations. This pattern of attacks was not different from South Africa's case which resulted into xenophobia in 2008. In Zambia, discontent and hostility towards foreigners by local residents resulted in xenophobia and made cultural integration almost impossible. This situation has made it difficult for foreigners to get assimilated in Zambia. Based on this background, this research is aimed at providing a deeper insight of xenophobia and its impact on cultural integration.

This research further attempts to show how a country's image gets dented after experiencing xenophobia. Thus, having this understanding is a critical step towards not only knowing impediments to cultural integration but also what needs to be done in order to promote cultural integration in a globalised world.

1.1 Scope of study This research develops an in-depth understanding of xenophobia in Zambia and its impact on cultural integration. It examines xenophobia and cultural integration from three distinctive areas of mediated messages, in-depth interviews (survey) and economic pressure in relation to xenophobia and culture integration. This research focuses on a period between April 2016 and June 2016 because this was the period in which xenophobia occurred and it also incorporates beliefs after this period to have a deeper understating of the impact of xenophobia.

2.0 Literature review
Polit et al (2001) maintains that literature review provides a background for understanding current knowledge on the topic. Therefore, this research provides synthesis of information regarding xenophobia, what it is and up to date information in order to understand the subject in more detail. Oxford advanced learners dictionary defines xenophobia as irrational hatred or fear of foreigners. Xenophobia is a severe aversion to foreigners, strangers and their cultures. It covers any kind of fear related to an individual or group perceived as being different from the person with the phobia.

Studies show that people with xenophobia do not accept that their condition is based on fear. In most cases, xenophobia is tied to nationalism and ethnocentrism both of which concepts are characterized by belief in the superiority of one's culture or national to another Schirmer (1998). Xenophobia has been around in many parts of the world and its very existence illuminates a weakness in the inter-relationships upon which society is founded.

Countries that have experienced xenophobia have been isolated and termed as nations of violence. In Southern Africa, South Africa is an example and Zambia being the second country to experience xenophobia in the recent past, joins South Africa being viewed in this light. Despite experiencing xenophobia for the first time, Zambia takes on the same image as those countries that have been involved in it for a longer period of time.

Akinola (2017) observed that the fact that Zambia has only experienced xenophobic attack once in its history does not exclude a country from the "Hall infamous and xenophobic states."Xenophobia is most common in countries with high number of foreigners and regions experiencing high migration.

In Southern Africa, migration has steadily increased and according to United Nations High Commission for Refugees UNHCR (2017) statistics, Zambia currently hosts about 58,000 refugees mostly from Angola, the Democratic Republic of the

Congo, Rwanda, Burundi, Somalia and Uganda. Along with this high number of foreigners, a rise in intolerance and animosity towards foreigners has been observed across all social areas in Zambia.

It's important to note that countries that have more foreigners are bound to experience a clash in cultural beliefs, values and norms as well as increased competition. This trend is not different from countries that have experienced xenophobia in the past. A good example is South Africa and Zambia now.

The increase of foreigners in the country brings along lot of challenges for cultural integration. Social scientists assert that countries where people of different races live, xenophobia and racism are ever present. However, the two phenomenon are quiet distinct in nature. Racism usually entails distinctions based on physical characteristic differences such as skin colour and other features, while xenophobia is based on the idea that the other person originates from outside the community or nation. This research focuses on xenophobia based on what was experienced in Zambia.

3.0 Methodology

This part of the research is aimed at providing the methodological approaches and research design for this study. This research adopts qualitative research in order to inquire, gather, analyse and interpret data collected for the purposes of research. Holloway and Wheeler (2002) refer to qualitative research as a form of social inquiry that focuses on the way people interpret and make sense of their experience and the world in which they live. Hence, this study uses qualitative research approach to explore behaviour, perspectives, experiences and trends. The method employed for this research involved interviews with foreigners, collection of news articles and a survey with local residents.

4.0 Findings

The main purpose of the research interview is to explore the views, experiences, beliefs or motivations of individuals on specific matters, Gill et.al (2008).Therefore, the rationale and logic behind using interviews was to explore opinions, perceptions and motivation to explain certain behaviour regarding xenophobia. Below are tables showing relevant data from interviews conducted with 24 foreigners from four different countries regarding xenophobia. The purpose of these interviews was to understand belief of foreigners whether they integrated culturally after xenophobia experience. An analysis of these interviews will subsequently follow.

Table 4.1: Respondents from Somalia

Nationality	Sex	Age	Period of Stay	Desire to leave	Language Spoken	Do you feel culturally part of Zambia after Xenophobia
Somalia	Female	25	12 Months	Yes	Foreign	No
	Female	24	24 months	Yes	Foreign	No
	Male	20	2 years	Yes	Foreign	No
	Male	35	6 months	Yes	Foreign	No
	Female	27	6 months	Yes	Host & foreign	Yes
	Male	27	9 months	Yes	Foreign	No

Source: Field Data 2017

Table 4.2: Respondents from Zimbabwe

Nationality	Sex	Age	Period of Stay	Desire to leave	Language Spoken	Do you feel culturally part of Zambia after Xenophobia
Zimbabwe	Female	25	3 Months	Yes	Host & foreign	No
	Female	24	7 Months	Yes	Foreign	Yes
	Male	24	1 year	No	Foreign	Sometimes
	Male	27	1 year	Yes	Foreign	No
	Male	25	2 years	Yes	Foreign	No
	Male	21	8 month	Yes	Foreign	No

Source: Field Data 2017

Table 4.3: Respondents from Rwanda

Nationality	Sex	Age	Period of Stay	Desire to leave	Language Spoken	Do you feel culturally part of Zambia after Xenophobia
Rwandan	Female	25	25 month	No	Host and foreign	Yes
	Female	24	8 Months	Yes	Foreign	No
	Male	23	2 years	Yes	Foreign	No
	Male	45	2 years	Yes	Foreign	No
	Male	33	2 years	Yes	Foreign	No
	Male	33	1 year	Yes	Foreign	No

Source: Field Data 2017

Table 4.4: Respondents from DR Congo

Nationality	Sex	Age	Period of Stay	Desire to leave	Language Spoken	Do you feel culturally part of Zambia after Xenophobia
Congolese	Female	25	9 month	Yes	Host & foreign	Yes
	Female	24	8 Months	Yes	Foreign	No
	Male	23	2 years	Yes	Foreign	No
	Male	45	2 years	No	Foreign	Undecided
	Male	33	2 years	Yes	Foreign	No
	Male	33	1 year	Yes	Foreign	No

Source: Field Data 2017

To explore further how news media covered xenophobia and how media house style, headlines and use of words dented the country's image thereby affecting cultural integration, this research presents selected stories that were reported during the period April to June 2016. An analysis of these news stories will subsequently follow. Below are excerpts from four online publications namely BBC, Lusaka Times, Allfrica, and The Mail and Guardian.

Zambia xenophobic riots: Two burned alive in Lusaka Two people were burned to death on Monday during xenophobic violence in Zambia's capital, Lusaka, police have said in a statement. The riots started after rumours that Rwandans were behind recent ritual killings in the city. The two were Zambian nationals killed "in the confusion" Home Affairs Minister Davies Mwila reportedly said. More than 250 people have been arrested after more than 60 Rwandan-owned shops were looted in two days of violence. The two Zambians had been burned with firewood and vehicle tyres, according to police quoted by the AFP news agency. Six people have been murdered since March and their body parts removed." Rumours circulated that the body parts would be used as charms to ensure success in business.

Source: BBC News 2016

Xenophobic attacks in Lusaka spread
Violent attacks targeted at foreign owned shops in Zingalume and George Compounds in Lusaka which broke out on Monday morning have spread to Garden and Mandevu areas. The riots started in Zingalume and George compound before engulfing parts of Lilanda but were quelled by police officers in riot gear. The protestors later stormed Kasungula road near Mandevu compound and started looting shops belonging to Rwandese nationals. They also entered Katimamulilo road near Garden compound accusing Rwandese nationals of being the recent killings in the area. The riots sporadically spread to Garden compound as many Rwandese nationals rushed to close their businesses and feared for their lives. The residents threw stones and other objects and chanted anti Government slogans and threatened to take their protests to State House. The rioters mostly got away with fridges, grocery items and beer from the shops they looted.

Source: Lusaka Times - 2016

Zambia: Tackling Xenophobia in Zambia
"Since independence, Zambia has never experienced such levels of xenophobic sentiments as witnessed recently against the Rwandese whose shops were looted in riots that spread to some townships in Lusaka. Although more than 250 people have been arrested in Lusaka to curb xenophobic violence, much civic education needs to be done for Zambians to learn to live in harmony with the Rwandese and other new arrivals like Lebanese and the Chinese. From media reports, at least 62 Rwandan-owned shops were looted in the riots, which are the worst xenophobic violence in the country. The riots started in two areas on Monday following rumours that Rwandans were behind ritual killings in Lusaka. This follows news of at least seven people being murdered in recent weeks and their body parts removed." Authorities should take the attacks that were ignited by rumours that Rwandese were behind the ritual killings seriously since the status quo of Zambia being a haven of peace for foreigners has been challenged.

Source: AllAfrica.com 2016

Hundreds arrested after xenophobic attacks erupt in Lusaka
Xenophobic attacks in Zambia's capital Lusaka continued on Tuesday with several foreign-owned shops broken into and looted by locals in the city's townships. The attacks that started on Monday in one of Lusaka's densely populated townships – Zingalume – spread to Ngombe, Kanyama, Chawama, Kalikiliki, Chunga, George and Matero townships. The riots were sparked by rumours that Rwandans were behind ritual killings. At least seven people have been murdered in recent weeks and their body parts removed, supposedly for muti or witchcraft. Police spokesperson Charity Munganga-Chanda on Tuesday confirmed the spread of the xenophobic attacks and said 62 shops had been looted, while 256 suspects had been arrested. When local media visited Chawama Tuesday morning, they found shopkeepers had closed their shops and some residents had stayed indoors. Following the attacks, panic and fear has gripped Lusaka residents because of the rise in ritual murders that have sparked riots and looting in several townships. On Monday, Lusaka residents from various compounds rioted over escalating ritual killings in Zingalume. Most shops belonging to Burundian and Rwandan nationals were broken into and goods looted, while all the shops owned by foreign nationals in many other townships that had not been looted, were found closed.

Source: The Mail and Guardian 2016

The above news excepts where taken from four different news online publications that reported about xenophobia in Zambia. The publications focused attention on xenophobia in the period under review. There was persistent news coverage of xenophobia by the publications and these are a combination of local and international online publications.

4.1 Economic performance

The period between 2015 and 2016 was challenging for Zambia economically. According to International Monetary Fund IMF Report (2016) indicates that lower copper prices, electricity shortages and poor rainfall dampened the pace of economic activities slowed by increased inflation. It added that a rise in expenditure pressures and financing conditions tightened sustainably. Furthermore, Monitoring Survey (2015) showed that inflation rate had gone up 17.6 per cent and unemployment reached 13.4 percent. These challenges resulted in 40.8 percent of people living in extreme poverty.

Despite, economic data reported by IMF and Monitory Survey on the cause of economic downturn, the reports did not have scientific merits to substantiate and explain the causes of the intense economic pressure especially in relation to the suffering of the majority of residents.

The majority of local residents believed economic problems were caused by foreigners building on the belief that, Zambia was considered a heaven for peace and opportunities for foreigners and that most of the foreigners who settled in Zambia were involved in business which deprived local residents opportunities. Furthermore, most foreigners found settlement and shelter in high density areas that were mainly characterised by high unemployment, lack of economic opportunities and extreme poverty, so competition for limited resources in these areas had been very intense disadvantaging local residents, thus a belief that foreigners were the causers of economic ills and extreme poverty.

A survey with 24 residents was conducted to find out their belief if foreigners contributed to economic problems, if foreigners businesses should be prevented, banned or if they should not be integrated. Below is data showing results of the survey.

Table 4.5: Survey with local residents

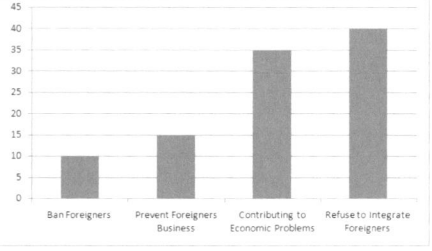

Source: Survey Data 2017

Through the survey, results show different views about the presence of foreigners. 10% of the respondents feel foreigners should be banned from doing business within certain localities, 15% interviewed indicated that foreigners needed to be prevented doing businesses whilst 35% showed that foreigners contributed to economic problems. 40% of the respondents refused to have foreigners integrated in Zambia.

5.0 Analyses

Given information and data, this research proceeds to analyse the data taking into account all different aspects.

5.1 Interviews with foreigners as respondents

In the first interview from tables 1, 2, 3 and 4 there were 24 foreigners interviewed as respondents through random and informal interviews. The sample space included 9 females and 15 males. All 9 females and 15 males were foreigners. From the data presented, 21 respondents expressed desire to leave the host country because of xenophobia and hostility towards foreigners experienced during the period of xenophobia. In addition, the respondents indicated that they would leave the host country for other countries provided they were culturally integrated in other countries. 3 respondents expressed no desire to leave the host county citing long period of stability in the host county. The desire by foreigners to leave the host country revealed high levels of difficulties for foreigners to culturally integrate in the host country.

In terms of languages spoken, 20 respondents preferred to use their own language with no interest of learning the host country's languages. The respondents indicated that this gave them a sense of belonging to their own culture. Lack of willingness to learn host country's languages created a barrier necessary for cultural integration. English was regarded as the common international language most foreigners used which was not used on a regular basis by most residents of host country. Only 4 respondents used both foreign and host country's languages.

From Table 1, Five out of six Somalians interviewed felt they were not culturally part of Zambia after xenophobia except 1 respondent. Despite respondents having stayed longer in the host country, most felt they could not be culturally integrated after the incident of xenophobia.

Respondents in Table 2 were Zimbabweans. Four out of six respondents interviewed felt they were not culturally integrated whilst one respondent felt was and another one felt was sometimes. Meanwhile, five respondents from Rwanda in Table 3 felt they could not be culturally integrated after xenophobia except for one respondent.

Respondents from Democratic Republic of Congo DRC in Table 4, only four respondents felt they could not be culturally integrated but one respondent felt was integrated with another one feeling undecided.

From the interview conducted, most respondents felt they could not be culturally integrated after xenophobia because the host country was not a safe place to live in and foreigners felt intimidated. The data from the interview reveal a pattern that show citizens from countries that were most affected by xenophobia like Somalia and Rwanda, had a high number of respondents that felt that they could not be culturally integrated after xenophobia.

5.2 News Sources

Selected news articles were used to monitor the direction of news coverage on xenophobia. Between April and June 2016, the tone of online media publications of stories about Xenophobia showed highly negative reporting. Coverage about xenophobia did not focus much on remedial process to xenophobia but about how the situation was worsening. The coverage started to move in a more positive direction only when government reacted to xenophobia. However, this was not enough to counteract negative publicity earlier.

The tone of the news coverage, style, format, words used about xenophobia were not neutral or even briefly positive, but the predominant coverage was persistently in the negative tone and use of screaming headlined that depicted the situation was worse for foreigners. The use of headlines like *"Zambia xenophobic riots: Two burned alive in Lusaka"* and *"Xenophobic attacks in Lusaka spread"* were too sensitive and negative in a sense which inherently showed the host country as a hostile place for foreigners with no room for cultural integration. Based on media logic theory which states that common media formats and styles serve as a means of perceiving the world. Thus, most people perceived the host country as unfriendly and hostile towards foreigners and immigrants. This kind of media reporting about xenophobia stood far from promoting cultural integration.

Furthermore, it is important to state that following media logic theory, people who read articles about xenophobia perceived Zambia in the negative light hence damaging the image of Zambia regarding foreigners. Although, Stuart Hall (1980) challenged this theory and argued that the power of the media is not absolute because people are not passive receivers of news. The main feature of this argument is expressed in Hall's model of preferred reading where it's indicated that audience enjoy the possibilities of alternatives. This is true but the extent to which stories were covered was enough evidence to suggest that people who might have read, seen or viewed these stories, chose them because there was no much alternatives to these stories.

Again, according to cultural theory which states that heavy exposure to media causes individuals to develop a perception of reality based on the most repetitive and consistent messages of a particular medium. This implies that people that repeatedly had access to online publications, read stories or saw what was happening regarding xenophobia and perceived the country in a negative light thereby denting the image of the country and perceived it as hostile towards other cultures.

5.3 Economic performance

Apart from media coverage, another compounding issue that contributed to xenophobia was economic pressure. According to data from World Bank and IMF, during 2015 and 2016 Zambia was under intense economic pressure and this was potential for unrest. Furthermore, the fact that local residents believed that economic pressures, competition and difficulties were caused by foreigners, this meant that local residents felt an increasing number of foreigners were having a larger part of the economic pie and disadvantaged them economically. According to Realistic Conflict theory by Sherif et.al (1961) explains that the conflict, negative prejudices, and discrimination occur between groups of people who are in competition for the same resources. This explains why residents of the host country were led to rise against foreigners.

In addition, a key feature of the survey with local residents is that 40% of the respondents showed refusal to integrate foreigners reflecting high opposition for cultural integration. 15% interviewed expressed feeling that that foreigners needed to be prevented from doing business whilst 35% indicated that foreigners contributed to economic problems that local people were facing. Only 10% of the respondents said foreigners should be banned from doing business within their localities.

The results from this survey explain how economic challenges are correlated to xenophobia and how this affects culture integration. This survey found virtues that do not tolerate or promote cultural integration from economic perspective. Based on this logic, xenophobia was motivated by a belief that economic problems were caused by the presence of foreigners hence making cultural integration impossible.

6.0 Findings and Conclusions

To summarize, this paper found a strong relationship between belief, mediated messages, economic pressure and cultural integrations. This paper discovered that beliefs, media coverage and economic pressure had a negative impact on cultural integration. These factors created barriers to cultural integration.

This research found that because Zambia went through xenophobia, beliefs and perceptions formed by foreigners made it difficulties for them to culturally integrate in the Zambian society coupled with their different cultural background. Data gathered and analysed showed that most foreigners did not feel culturally integrated after xenophobia occurred. Despite some foreigners having lived in Zambia even long before xenophobia occurred in 2016, had their belief changed after xenophobia that Zambia was a heaven for foreigners. This change in belief and perception made cultural integration difficult and by the logic of this analysis, beliefs and perception as a result of xenophobia affected cultural integration.

All foreigners interviewed, data showed that more foreigners were willing to leave Zambia for other countries because they found it difficult to culturally integrate as xenophobia created fear, uncertainty and isolation. These factors further created huge cultural distance between foreigners and residents of the host country thereby threatening cultural integration. In addition, few foreigners did not attempt to speak languages of the host country to help them integrate easily but opted to use their own languages so they could identify and associate easily with people from their countries. This unwillingness to learning to speak languages of the host country affected cultural integration because it created a barrier.

Some foreigners also revealed that residents of the host country preferred them to assimilate to the host country's culture, leaving their own cultural heritage behind. This confirms most scholarly studies that have shown that residents of the host country tend to prefer that foreigners and immigrants assimilate and adopt culture of the host country and abandon their own.

This research found that this was the case in Zambia, but over a period of time such preferences resulted in increased cultural division and isolation of foreigners as most of them did not embrace it. Most foreigners attempted to hold on to their sense of cultural identity than adopting the culture of the host country. This clash created cultural barriers between foreigners and residents of the host country thereby creating difficulties for cultural integration.

Differences in accepting another ones culture were rooted in xenophobia experienced in the periods of xenophobia.

In terms of media coverage, news content, coverage, tone and focus on xenophobia during the period of study showed a prolonged negative pattern of xenophobia by most publications.

Furthermore, this consistent news coverage to the public meant that news received by the public was predominately negative. Negative news coverage about xenophobia created beliefs and perceptions that plausibly contributed towards public disaffection of Zambia's cultural relations with foreigners and immigrants. This further affected cultural integration.

There is reasonable theoretical evidence that the media have power to influence people's perception and attitudes as one of the many socializing agents. Thus, media coverage of xenophobia during the period dented the image of Zambia. Akinola (2017) states that although Zambia is not renowned for xenophobic occurrences, reports have confirmed its prevalence among masses and the 2016 violence against immigrants dented the country's imagine as a heaven for refugees and other categories of immigrants. This image created poses as a threat to culture integration and this explains why people no longer look at Zambia as a beacon of peace and heaven for immigrants.

Research and other theoretical findings show that xenophobia in most cases is predicated and followed by long periods of difficult economic times that countries go through such as high unemployment, lack of economic opportunities and extreme poverty. According to Economist Intelligence Unit (2015) Zambia was ranked among the hungriest countries on the Global Hunger Index GHI. In addition, Tshitereke (1999) found that hostilities toward foreign nationals were in relation to limited resources. Therefore, this research found that periods of intense economic pressure was a predicate to xenophobia in Zambia as was the case in South Africa. This observation helps explain why attacks on foreigners in Zambia were followed by looting of goods belonging to foreigners.

This is a common phenomenon in countries that have experienced xenophobia. Theoretical studies show that foreigners and immigrants became "frustration-scapegoat" and targets to blame for deprivation and extreme poverty.

Furthermore, a survey conducted show that residents of the host country developed hostility towards foreigners in periods of intense economic problems and blamed it on foreigners. The survey provides reasons to believe that economic downturn are a predicate to xenophobia.

This research found that as a result of xenophobia, foreigners felt isolated, intimidated, and socially detached. They perceived the host county as hostile, violent and unwelcome to other cultures the elements of which are among the main factors that affect culture integration. Xenophobia created beliefs shared among almost all foreigners that Zambia was no longer a safe place for foreigners to stay thereby difficult to culturally integrate.

Therefore, based on these findings, the impact of xenophobia on cultural integration can be conceptualized in terms of beliefs, economic problems and mediated messages as factors that created threats and barriers to cultural integration in Zambia. Thus this research recommends a need for economic improvement, change in mediated messages about xenophobiaand avoidance of prejudice against foreigners as means to prevent xenophobia and promote cultural integration.

Reference

Oksana Yakushko (2009) Xenophobia: Understanding the Roots andConsequences of Negative Attitudes towardImmigrants.

Tapiwa Gomo (2009) Analysis of media reporting and xenophobia violence among youth in South Africa.

Randy Thornhill, Corey L. Fincher (2014),the Parasite-Stress Theory of Values and Sociality: Infectious Disease, History and Human Values Worldwide.

Akinola, Adeoye O. (2017),the Political Economy of Xenophobia in Africa.

The Economist Intelligence Unit EIU (2016). Xenophobic violence erupts after spate of murders. London: EIU

United Nations High Commission for Refugees UNHCR (2016). Figures at aglance. Geneva: UNHCR. Available at *www.unhcr.org/figures-at-a-glance.html*.

United Nations High Commission for Refugees (UNHCR). 2009. Global

Trends2009. Geneva: UNHCR. *Available at www.unhcr.org*.

United Nations High Commissioner for Refugees UNHCR Report (2015)*Available at www.unhcr.org*.

United Nations High Commission for Refugees (UNHCR). 2016. Statistics: theWorld in Numbers. *Available at www.unhcr.org*.

University of Minnesota Media Effects Theories by is licensed under a Creative Commons Attribution.

http://placebrandobserver.com/theory/place-image-reputation/

Methods of data collection in qualitative research: interviews and focus groups P. Gill, 1 K. Stewart,2 E. Treasure 3 and B. Chadwick 4

YOUR KNOWLEDGE HAS VALUE

- We will publish your bachelor's and master's thesis, essays and papers

- Your own eBook and book - sold worldwide in all relevant shops

- Earn money with each sale

Upload your text at www.GRIN.com
and publish for free